BIBLE STUDY WORKBOOK

Beautiful You!
(Inside and Out!)

A Study for Women on the Book of Esther
—And so Much More!

❖ *Find your real identity in Christ*

❖ *Be released from past bondages*

❖ *Develop a beautiful and confident*
inner self and exterior presence

Lisa Veach

WESTBOW
PRESS®
A DIVISION OF THOMAS NELSON
& ZONDERVAN

WestBow Press books may be ordered through booksellers or by contacting:

WestBow Press
A Division of Thomas Nelson & Zondervan
1663 Liberty Drive
Bloomington, IN 47403
www.westbowpress.com
1 (866) 928-1240

ISBN: 978-1-9736-2862-0 (sc)
ISBN: 978-1-9736-2863-7 (e)

Library of Congress Control Number: 2018905897

Print information available on the last page.

WestBow Press rev. date: 8/27/2018

Contents

Acknowledgments

I wish to thank a number of people who helped make this study book and its companion possible.

Thank you to Annie Addington, Sarah Cruz, and Ashley Weeks Clark, all of whom approached me with the desire to have some type of study aid for young women.

I appreciate the encouragement and guidance of writers Judy Dipple, Patricia Marshall, Midge Raymond, and Dean Rea as I tried to navigate through this new venture of writing.

I appreciate David Veach giving a little of his valuable time to help Mom out on a new computer system!

I appreciate Marissa and Sarah Arroyo and Cara Taylor helping me with a few technical components on the computer.

Thanks so much to R. B. May for some editorial and technical assistance.

Thank you to Cindy Birkinshaw, Barbara Carse, and Gloria Hawkins for taking the time to read and make constructive comments. You and your comments are appreciated!

I greatly appreciate Debra Norland's careful reading and valuable editing comments. Thank you so much for your copious time and expertise! Debra, you helped me finish this book and its companion. Thank you so much!

Teresa Madson, from Christian Discount Books in Jacksonville, Oregon, graciously allowed me to purchase and borrow some books in order to retrieve some extra information that I needed for publishing. Thank you, Teresa!

Thank you to Jason Addington and Ashley Childs for graciously and generously giving of your time and expert computer advice so I could finish the books. I so appreciate the help you both gave me. Jason, I could not have done this without you! Thank you so much!

I appreciate the staff at WestBow Press for all their assistance. This includes Tim Fitch, Venus Gamboa, and my editors. I greatly appreciate the refining input given by these editors.

Special appreciation goes to Eric Schroeder and Jordan Ling, both from WestBow Press. Mr. Schroeder answered numerous questions quickly, with accuracy, and with a positive helpful attitude. Mr. Ling was a valuable editorial asset. I appreciate the time, clarity and graciousness with which he answered my questions. Thank you so much!

I greatly appreciate all the love and support from my husband, Aaron. He read through the manuscript several times, making numerous editing comments. When these were complete, he designed several new ways to format the material. Thank you, Aaron, for all your emotional, intellectual, and hands-on support! You made the difference in completing this Bible study.

Of course, the most important One to thank is our wonderful Lord, without whom this would not have been written. He is the one who created all of us. He is the one who gives the inspiration and equipping for each task. He is the one who knows when each book is to be written and whose lives it will touch. May this touch your life and do all that He desires to accomplish!

To God be the glory!
Lisa Veach

Preface

Shortly after my husband and I were called to a new pastorate, I became aware that most of the young ladies in that church had low self-esteem and a poor self-image. As I prayed for these ladies in their teens and twenties, God gave me the idea of a creative study on the book of Esther. Because I was the director of music and also taught a young couples class, the study did not materialize at that time. Some years later, several youth leaders came to me with the same concern I had observed. They asked for ideas as to how to help the young ladies. God again brought back to my mind this study on Esther.

This study has several lesson topics specifically for younger single ladies, but they are presented in such a way as to be beneficial for women of all ages.

Esther's identity was strongly rooted in her faith in God and the *agape* love of her cousin, Mordecai. Because of her own self-image as a servant of God and her faith in Him, she became a beautiful woman inside and out. This resulted in God's use of her to accomplish a dangerous and critical task for Him and His people.

As women (and men), we will find our true identities and God-ordained purposes in a relationship of love and obedience with the God who created us.

It is my hope and prayer that this study will be a tool God uses to help mentors of women and youth leaders guide ladies of various ages to discover:

❖ who we really are in Christ;
❖ how to grow and learn to walk with Him in a relationship of love, trust, and obedience; and
❖ how to develop the full potential of womanhood Christ has put within us.

I am well aware that this is not a definitive work on the many areas addressed in this study. I pray it will lay a good foundation, along with a strong infrastructure, from which women will continue to grow:

❖ in Christ,
❖ in their own self-identity, and
❖ in their relationships with others.

I pray women will be set free from past hurts and injustices, becoming whole in Christ and discovering and fulfilling the God-ordained purposes for which they were created.

Praying God's healing and growth on all who enter into this study,

Lisa Veach

Lesson 1

Introduction

Welcome to this special study just for women, based on the life of Esther.
During this lesson, we will:

- have some fun icebreakers to facilitate becoming better acquainted;
- watch a DVD on Esther, the heroine of our study;[1] and
- find out the purpose of this study.

God loves each one of you. He sees your strengths, He sees your weaknesses, and He sees your pain. Just as He helped Esther, who is our biblical heroine, overcome the pain of her childhood, He wants a personal relationship with you. He wants to heal you. He wants you to be an overcomer. He has a purpose, plan, and destiny for your life, tailor-made just for you.

You have been invited to be a part of Esther's legacy:

- ❖ to learn to walk with God in a loving, trusting, obedient relationship;
- ❖ to learn to turn *to* Him with problems, questions, doubts, and decisions;
- ❖ to learn to overcome the hurts and wrongs done to you;
- ❖ to learn to become a beautiful woman of God, inside and out; and
- ❖ to fulfill your God-given destiny.

This is the purpose of the study.

During the week take some time to read the short book of Esther.
Next week, please bring your Bible and a pen or pencil. We will dive in and start to learn some things from Esther's life that will help us become beautiful, fulfilled women of God.

Lesson 2

Why Jesus?

Understanding the Setting of Esther

Read Esther 1:1–9.

1. Where did this story take place?

2. In what city did this story take place (1:2, 5)?

3. When did this take place?

How Is Jesus Linked to Esther?

1. What nationality was Esther (2:5–7)?

2. What nation is made up of Jews?

3. What nationality was Jesus (Matt. 27:27–29)?

4. In this story, whom did Haman want to annihilate (Esther 3:13)?

5. Because Jesus was a Jew, if all these Jews had been killed, is it possible that He might not have been born?

God could have brought about the forgiveness of our sins through any avenue He desired. He chose to create the nation of Israel so that Jesus would come through them and offer humankind forgiveness of sins and a restored relationship with God.

What Did Jesus Do for Us?

1. Read Romans 3:23. What do we learn from this scripture?

2. Read Romans 6:23. What does this mean?

3. Read Romans 5:8.
    a. Why did He die to pay for our sins?

    b. What should our response be to such love?

How Do I Become a Child of God?

God has a specific way for us to become His child, make Him our Lord, and be forgiven. We will study some scriptures that will help us understand the process.

1. Read John 3:5–6, Acts 2:38, and Galatians 4:6. What do the following two terms mean?
    a. "Born of Water"

b. "Born of the Spirit"

2. Let's look at two scriptures on baptism.
   a. Read Acts 2:38. What do we learn from this scripture?

   b. Read Romans 6:4. Explain the meaning of Romans 6:4 combined with Acts 2:38.

3. Let's look at two other scriptures concerning a new life in Christ.
   a. Read 2 Corinthians 5:15. What do we learn from this scripture?

   b. Read Revelation 3:20. What do we learn about Jesus from this scripture?

*Would you like to ask God into your heart, be baptized, be forgiven of all
your sins, and have a new purpose, that of living for Christ?
Any time you feel God speak to you, wanting you to accept Him, that's God's Spirit
saying, "I want you to be part of My family." That is your time to decide.*

You and Your Life Are Important to God

Let's read four more scriptures that show how important you and your life are to God.

1. Read Psalm 139:13–18. What does this scripture reveal about you and about God?

2. Read Psalm 56:8. What does this scripture reveal about God?

3. Read John 16:33. What does this scripture reveal about our lives and about God?

We will have trouble in this world. It is one of the consequences of Adam and Eve's choice to turn from God and live life their way. As a result, there is evil in this world. God knows we will get hurt by the evil that other people do, but He says, "Come to Me, trust Me. I have lived on this earth victoriously, and I will help you do it also!"

4. Read Isaiah 43:1–2.
   a. What do you think "the rivers" and "the fire" refer to?

   b. Keeping this is mind, what do you learn from Isaiah 43:1–2 about God and about His care for Israel and for you?

   c. Why does He care for us?

A relationship with God is the basis for the best self-image a person can have. It is also the basis for discovering who we are in our Creator's eyes, and the potential He sees in us. Through the power of His Holy Spirit, we will be able to overcome every hurt and difficulty life throws at us. We will also be able to accomplish all that God has in store for us.

This week we studied really hard. Next week, come prepared to study more about Esther and to party! Sign up to bring your favorite party food!

Lesson 3

Party Time!

There are three banquets, or parties, in the first chapter of Esther. Today we will study the first two. Let's begin with the first banquet.

The First Banquet

Read Esther 1:1–4.

1. Where was the first banquet held (1:2)?

2. Who gave the banquet (1:2–3)?

3. How long had he been reigning when he gave it (1:3)?

4. For whom did King Ahasuerus give the banquet (1:3)?

5. Why did he give it (1:4)?

6. Was he valuing others or himself?

7. Read Philippians 2:3–4. What do we learn from this scripture?

8. How long did the king's banquet last (Esther 1:4)?

9. How many months is that?

10. And what was his purpose again?

The Second Banquet

Read Esther 1:5–8.

1. For whom was this banquet given (1:5)?

2. Who hosted this banquet (1:5)?

3. Why do you think he did this?

4. Do you think he gave them a banquet because he really cared about them?

Jesus's Heart toward Us

1. Does Jesus treat us the way King Ahasuerus treated his people?

   a. Read Matthew 11:28–30. What does this scripture reveal about Jesus?

   b. Read Isaiah 40:11. To whom is this passage referring?

Jesus is pictured as the good, perfect shepherd who takes care of us, His sheep.

      1)   What four things does Jesus do in this passage of scripture for His flock (us)?

          a)

          b)

          c)

          d)

This is how God loves and cares for us. He has a pure heart of love for us.

God's agape *love demonstrates desiring the best for us and for others.*

Riches: Something to Value?

   1.   How do we know that King Ahasuerus was very rich (Esther 1:4–7)?

      a.

      b.

      c.

      d.

e.

f.

2. How do most people feel about riches and the people who have them?

3. Read James 1:10–11 and Matthew 6:19–21 to discover God's view concerning riches.
   a. What do these two passages teach us about God's view of riches and rich people?

   1)

   2)

   3)

   b. What does God want us to value?

Prayerfully consider: What does my heart value?

Lesson 4

Characteristics of Love

The Third Banquet

The third banquet, or party, was Queen Vashti's. She gave it in King Ahasuerus's palace for the women.

Read Esther 1:9–22.

1. What did the king command Queen Vashti to do during her banquet (1:10–11)?

2. Why was Vashti ordered to come (1:11)?

3. Why did she refuse to come?

4. What are some of the things the American people value?

5. Read Micah 6:8 to discover some of God's values. What are the three things listed here that God values?

    a.

    b.

    c.

6. How did the king react to Vashti's refusal to come (1:12)?

7. Why do you think the king was angry?

   a.

   b.

8. Did the king respond to Queen Vashti's refusal to come to him in a mature or immature way (1:12–22)? Explain.

9. Why do you think Memucan said that Queen Vashti's actions were wrong and would cause other women to rise up and disrespect their husbands (1:16–20)?

10. How did he propose to keep order (1:19–22)?

    a.

    b.

Godly Expressions of Love

How does the Bible say husbands and wives should treat one another?

1. Read Ephesians 5:21, 25, and 33.

2. Explain the meaning of the phrase "Christ loved the church and gave Himself up for her" (Ephesians 5:25).

Godly Characteristics of Love in a Husband

Read 1 Corinthians 13:4–8a. Beginning with 1 Corinthians 13:4–8a and ending with Ephesians 5:25, list one characteristic of a godly husband after each number. After each characteristic, explain how a husband could show that characteristic.

1.

2.

3.

4.

5.

6.

7.

8.

9.

10.

11.

12.

13.

14.

15.

16.

Characteristics of King Ahasuerus

Were these the characteristics shown by King Ahasuerus?

Using these same scriptures, 1 Corinthians 13:4–8a and Ephesians 5:25, list the characteristics King Ahasuerus displayed. Explain how he showed each characteristic.

1.

2.

3.

4.

5.

6.

7.

8.

9.

10.

11.

12.

13.

14.

15.

16.

Godly Characteristics of Love in My Life

List a characteristic of love from 1 Corinthians 13:4–8a and Ephesians 5:25 after each number. Then write down how each characteristic could be put into practice in your own life.

1.

2.

3.

4.

5.

6.

7.

8.

9.

10.

11.

12.

13.

14.

15.

16.

God wants us to have the attributes of love listed in 1 Corinthians 13:4–8a.

Developing these attributes includes the following steps:

1) *Asking the Holy Spirit to develop them in us, and being sensitive to His corrective nudges when we blow it.*
2) *When we do blow it, asking for forgiveness from God and all involved.*
3) *Asking God to give us a plan for handling a similar situation in the future in a way that honors Him. This is a key point: we need to prayerfully plan how to handle a similar situation in the future in a way that honors God.*

An Important Characteristic of Love for Wives

Read Ephesians 5:22.

1. What does this scripture encourage wives to do?

2. What do you think this means?

*To be subject or submissive to a husband means
to come under his protection and headship.*

*When a husband is being the loving, godly man God desires,
the wife feels protected and cherished. She does not feel
controlled, but she feels very safe, fulfilled, and loved.*

*If you are in a difficult marriage, seek help from our Lord and a Christian counselor.
Allow God to transform you, even if your prince has turned into
a frog with warts. You are responsible for you, not him.*

*Ask God to transform you into a godly lady by spending time in His Word,
and by asking His Holy Spirit to change your thinking and reacting.*

Lesson 5

Agape

The Party Is Over

1. Esther 2:1 starts, "After these things ..." What does "after these things" refer to?

    a. Esther 1:3, 5, 9

    b. Esther 1:10–11

    c. Esther 1:12

    d. Esther 1:12

    e. Esther 1:13– 20

    f. Esther 1:21–22

2. After the banquets are over, life has returned to normal, and the king has gotten over his anger, what happens (Esther 2:1)?

    a. What is the plan his servants suggest (2:2–4)?

19

    b.   Does the servants' plan agree with God's design for marriage?

Marriage and Divorce

Let's read two passages from the Bible concerning marriage and divorce.

1.   Read Matthew 19:3–9. Why doesn't God want you to divorce?

2.   Read Proverbs 5:18–19. What do we learn from this scripture about marriage?

3.   Why do you think we should we work toward a good marriage instead of choosing to divorce? (The leader will have some supplemental answers.)

    a.

    b.

    c.

    d.

Esther's Self-image

1.   Read Esther 2:5–7 and explain what Esther's childhood was like.

2.   How do you think it would affect you if both of your parents were killed when you were young?

3. Every person reacts to loss or tragedy differently. What are some of the ways Esther could have been affected? (The leader will also have some items for this list.)

   a.

   b.

   c.

   d.

   e.

4. Keeping these things in mind, read Esther 2:8–9.

   a. Does Esther seem to be clinging, showing great insecurities or hysteria?

   b. What were Hegai's feelings toward her (2:8–9)?

   c. If she had been hysterical or clingy, had an emotional wall, or had no self-esteem, do you think she would have pleased him or won his favor?

5. Read Esther 2:12–15 and try to discern three things about Esther that may have pleased Hegai. Explain your answers.

   a.

   b.

c.

6. In Esther 2:15, we learn that Esther found favor with everyone.

    a. If Esther was physically beautiful but had a proud, haughty spirit, do you think she would have found favor in the eyes of everyone?

    b. If she was proud and arrogant, would the other women have liked her?

    c. Don't you think there should have been some resentment and jealousy toward Esther because of her beauty?

    d. Because there were only positive feelings toward Esther, what does this indicate about her?

    e. Esther was a beautiful woman, yet she seemed to be kind and considerate of others, instead of arrogant and self-absorbed. What do you think caused her to be this way?

7. Read the following scriptures and explain how you think Esther became a secure, lovely, teachable young lady after the trauma of being orphaned.

    a. Esther 2:5–7

    b. Esther 2:11

    c. Esther 4:14

Mordecai's statement—"And who knows whether you have not come to the kingdom for such a time as this?"—shows a wisdom and perspective that comes from not just believing in God but also walking with Him in a relationship.

He modeled his faith to Esther by both his teaching and his life.

Consider: What set Esther apart from the other women?

Joseph the Jew: His Coat of Many Colors and His Difficult Life

Read Genesis 39:1–3, 20–23.

1. Joseph had terrible things happen to him. He was sold as a slave to Potiphar. Then he was put in jail on a false charge of rape. Yet the Bible says, "The Lord was with Joseph." What does the phrase "The Lord was with Joseph" mean?

2. Consider all the following bad things that happened to Joseph:
    a. His brothers hated him.
    b. His brothers plotted to kill him but instead sold him into slavery.
    c. He repeatedly did what was right, though continually tempted by Potiphar's wife.
    d. Potiphar's wife lied about him when he was honorable.
    e. Potiphar had him thrown in jail on false charges, and he stayed there for years.
    f. The butler, who was supposed to help get him out of jail, forgot him even though Joseph had helped him.

Would you be bitter, hateful, and angry if your family or others had done this to you? Would you be angry if others in the world treated you wrongly, especially if you had only done what was right? How did Joseph keep from becoming bitter or distrustful of God?

Developing a Godly Perspective on Pain and Evil

Read Isaiah 55:8–9 and Genesis 45:4–8 to discover some things that may have helped Joseph avoid getting bitter or distrustful of God and enabled him to forgive his family.

1. List five things Joseph seemed to have done that helped him maintain his trust in God and forgive his family.

    a.

    b.

    c.

    d.

    e.

2. How can we avoid getting bitter and angry with God when life throws us a curve?

    a.

    b.

    c.

    d.

Whether or not you understand God's purpose, focus on Christ instead of the difficulties. Trust Him. Focusing on Him and trusting Him will help you:

1) *become more aware of His loving, caring presence;*
2) *love Him more;*
3) *realize that loving and serving Him should be your number one priority;*
4) *realize how powerful He is (because He is all-powerful and is able to help you, in time He will provide insight and direction for you); and*
5) *experience His great peace, joy, and fulfillment, even in the midst of a difficult circumstance.*

Esther and Mordecai's Example

1. Do you see Esther and Mordecai following the first three steps Joseph took in dealing with his difficulties?

2. Using the following scriptures, describe how Esther and/or Mordecai followed those steps.

   a. Esther 4:15–17

   b. Esther 4:13–14

   c. Esther 4:16

3. Why do you think Esther was willing to do this life-threatening request?

   a.

   b.

We need to be seeking God's will in everything.

4. What was underlying Esther's desire to follow in the footsteps of faith that her cousin had modeled for her?

Agape

There are four Greek words translated into the English Bible as *love*. These are:

1. *storge*

2. *eros*

3. *phileo*

4. *agape*

Agape is putting another's best interests ahead of your own because you love the person so much.

Agape is what Jesus showed us.

a. How would you feel toward a person who showed you this type of *agape* love by caring and taking time for you?

b. Would you feel that the person's input in teaching and guidance would be in your best interest?

c. Mordecai told Esther to tell no one of her identity as a Jew (Esther 2:10). Why did she obey him?

This self-sacrificing, this seeking the highest good of the other person, this agape *is the type of love God wants His people to have for Him and others.*

God has written you His love letter in the Bible. Will you read it?

Lesson 6

A Beautiful Fragrance

External Beautification

Read Esther 2:12–14.

1.   How long did the women prepare in their beauty regime before they went to the king (2:12)?

2.   How did they prepare (2:12)?

3.   Where is much of the focus in US beauty pageants?

4.   What would happen if you were "embalmed" in myrrh and spices for one year?

Transformed into a Beautiful Fragrance

Read 2 Corinthians 2:14. What do we learn from this scripture?

Transformed into a Beautiful Fragrance by Accepting Christ as Your Savior

How do we get to the point of having Christ's fragrance flow from us?

1. Read Acts 2:38. What do we learn from this scripture?

2. Read Romans 8:14. What do we discover from this scripture?

Transformed into a Beautiful Fragrance by the Renewal of Your Mind

How do we work with the Holy Spirit and "hear" from Him so that we can do as He asks?

1. Read Romans 12:2. What may we learn from this scripture?

2. Read Romans 8:5. How do we renew our minds?

3. What can we do to get our thoughts on the things of God instead of the things of this world?

> *Listen for the voice of the Spirit of God speaking to your heart. Then line up your heart and actions with what He and His Word say.*

Transformed into a Beautiful Fragrance through Relationships with Other Christians

Our transformation involves both our private relationship with God and our relationships with others. Read Hebrews 10:23–25. List the behaviors that are encouraged in this passage.

1.

2.

3.

4.

When we are down, other Christians can help lift us up. When they are down, we can help lift them up through words of encouragement, acts of kindness, and prayer. As we intercede in prayer, the Holy Spirit works in remarkable ways!

Transformed into a Beautiful Fragrance through Prayer

Prayer is a very important part of our transformation. It is one way we communicate with God, and He communicates with us. Read Ephesians 6:18. What four things do we learn regarding prayer?

1.

2.

3.

4.

We need to pray in accordance with God's will and through the power of His Spirit.

Nothing is too small or unimportant for God.

Transformed into a Beautiful Fragrance through Love and Obedience to God

Read John 14:21 to find another element that affects our transformation. What do we discover from this scripture?

1.

2.

When you know God has instructed you to do something— perform a task, give up a habit, or forgive—do as He says. His Spirit will speak to your heart, instructing you. He will give you the power to do what He has asked through His Holy Spirit. This is how you grow and move with Him. If you refuse, you will remain stuck. You will fail to become all that Christ wants you to be. Listen and cooperate with God. He knows best.

Review: Transformed into a Beautiful Fragrance

In conclusion, use the following scriptures and write down what we need to do in order to work with the Holy Spirit and let Him transform us so we are a pleasing fragrance for Him.

1. Acts 2:38

2. Romans 12:2

3. Ephesians 6:18

4. John 14:21

5. Hebrews 10:23–25

This is how we learn to let God transform us so His fragrance can flow from us to others.

Transformed into a Beautiful Fragrance through Your Quiet Time with God

A profitable quiet time with God may involve:
1. worship,
2. prayer (including writing out troubling areas, and listening for and writing out answers),
3. studying a book from the Bible and writing out what God says and teaches you, and
4. memorizing scriptures.

Let God guide your time with Him. He knows you and your needs.

Winning the King's Favor

Read Esther 2:13. What items do you think the maidens took with them to the king's palace to try to win his favor?

1.

2.

3.

4.

5.

    a. Do these items seem to have won his favor?

    b. What or who seemed to win his favor?

    c. Why do you think she won his favor?

    d. Do you think Esther would have been chosen if she had gone to the king without the proper beauty treatments, her hair uncombed, and her clothes a wrinkled mess?

Color Analysis

1. What is color analysis?[2]

2. The book *Color Me Beautiful* by Carole Jackson categorized women into four main categories: Winter, Summer, Autumn, and Spring.[3]

3. Here are some hints that may help you determine which season you are.
    a. Winter and Summer people look best in colors that have a cool palette. Winters look great in either blue-based colors or clear, true colors. They also look good in icy (a hint of) colors of the same shade. Winters are the only season that can wear black and pure white well. Summers look best in clear or softer muted colors that have either blue, rose, or gray undertones. These colors are less intense than the ones Winters wear. For example, a Winter will wear royal purple, whereas a Summer will wear plum, which is a muted purple.[4]

b. A Winter usually has stronger coloring with greater contrasts in skin, hair, and eyes. Summers are softer and less intense in their coloring. Because of the undertones, Winter and Summer are the cool palettes.[5]

c. Autumn's colors are based on golden tones, whereas Spring's colors have a clear, yellow undertone. They are the warm palettes. Autumn's palette is strong, with both vivid and muted colors. Only Autumns look great in orange and olive, but they don't wear navy, pink, or gray. Springs look best in clear colors that are either bright or delicate but never muted or extremely dark. They can wear a little of every yellowed color, but not black or pure white. Their white is a cream or yellowish white.[6]

d. Within the warm palette, Autumns have the more vivid coloring, whereas Springs are the softer counterpart.[7]

e. One more hint: If you tan easily, you are probably of the cool palette. If you burn easily and need sunscreen, you are most likely of the warm palette.

4. Let's take time now to decide whether you are of the warm or cool palate. Look at the charts on the next two pages and circle the characteristics that best describe you. This will help you discover which season you are. You may wish to discuss this with the other women.

5. Once you have decided your season, we will come back together for the last segment.

6. The information contained in Tables 1–4 is found on pages 47, 49, 51, and 53 of *Color Me Beautiful* by Carole Jackson.[8]

Winter

Table 1: Winter's Coloring

Skin	Hair	Eyes
Very white	Blue-black	Dark red-brown
White with delicate pink tone	Dark brown (may have red highlights)	Black-brown
Beige (no cheek color) may be sallow	Medium ash brown	Hazel (brown plus green or blue)
Gray-beige or brown	Salt-and-pepper	Gray-blue
Rosy beige	Silver-gray	Blue with white flecks in iris (may have a gray rim)
Olive	White blonde (rare)	Dark blue, violet
Black (blue undertone)	White	Gray-green
Black (sallow)		Green with white flecks in iris (may have a gray rim)

Summer

Table 2: Summer's Coloring

Skin	Hair	Eyes
Pale beige with delicate pink cheeks	Platinum blonde	Blue (with white webbing in the iris, cloudy look)
Pale beige with no cheek color (even sallow)	Ash blonde (often towhead as a child)	Green (with white webbing in the iris, cloudy look)
Rosy beige	Warm ash blonde (slightly golden)	Soft gray-blue
Very pink	Dark ash ("mouse") blonde	Soft gray-green
Gray-brown	Ash ("mouse") brown	Bright, clear blue
Rosy brown	Dark brown (taupe tone)	Pale, clear aqua (eyes change from blue to green depending on clothes)
	Brown with auburn cast	Hazel (cloudy brown smudge with blue or green)
	Blue-gray	Pale gray
	Pearl white	Soft rose-brown
		Grayed brown

Autumn

Table 3: Autumn's Coloring

Skin	Hair	Eyes
Ivory	Red	Dark brown
Ivory with freckles (usually redhead)	Coppery red-brown	Golden brown
Peach	Auburn	Amber
Peach with freckles (usually golden blonde, brown)	Golden brown (dark honey)	Hazel (golden brown, green gold)
Golden beige (no cheek color, needs blush)	Golden blonde (honey)	Green (with brown or gold flecks)
Dark beige (coppery)	Ash ("dirty") blonde	Pale, clear green
Golden brown	Strawberry blonde	Olive green
	Charcoal brown or black	Blue with a distinct aqua or turquoise tone
	Golden gray	Teal blue
	Oyster white	Steel blue

Spring

Table 4: Spring's Coloring

Skin	Hair	Eyes
Creamy ivory	Flaxen blonde	Blue with white "rays"
Ivory with pale golden freckles	Yellow blonde	Clear blue
Peach	Honey blonde	Steel blue
Peach/pink (may have pink/purple knuckles)	Strawberry blonde (usually with freckles)	Green with golden flecks
Golden beige	Strawberry redhead (usually with freckles)	Clear green
Rosy cheeks (may blush easily)	Auburn	Aqua
Golden brown	Golden brown	Teal
	Red-black (rare)	Golden brown
	Dove gray	
	Creamy white	

7. We are going to take a little more time to do something called color draping.[9] This involves draping one solid color of fabric at a time around a woman's neck and over her shoulders. Only the draped fabric should be near her face. The correct seasonal colors should make the woman's face "come alive." This needs to be done in natural or incandescent lighting.[10]

8. Once you determine your season, you will realize that you can wear almost any color. It's simply the shade—a blue-red (cool), or an orange or yellowed-red (warm),—and the intensity of those shades (vivid or softer) that will cause you to shine and look your very best![11] Let's look at the following chart to see which colors and shades of those colors will make you look your best.

9. The information contained in Table 5 will clearly show what colors look good on each season.[12]

Table 5: Seasonal Color Chart

Color	Winter	Summer	Autumn	Spring
White	Pure white	Soft white	Oyster white	Ivory
Beige	Gray-beige, (taupe), icy taupe	Rose beiges	Earth beiges, gold-tone, beiges, camel	Clear beiges, creamy beiges, camel
Gray	True grays, from icy to charcoal	Blue-grays, light to medium	No gray	Warm (yellow) grays, light to medium
Brown	No brown, no tan	Rose-browns, cocoa	Dark brown, most browns and tans (coffee, bronze, mahogany)	Golden browns, clear tans
Black	Black	No black	No black	No black
Navy	Any navy	Grayed navy	No navy	Clear light navy
Blue	True blue, royal blue, icy blue	Gray-blue, denim, sky blue, periwinkle blue, powder to medium blue	Teal blue, deep periwinkle	Light royal blue, periwinkle blues, light to dark
Turquoise	Hot turquoise, Chinese blue, icy aqua	Pastel aqua	Turquoise	Medium-warm turquoise, clear aqua

Color	Winter	Summer	Autumn	Spring
Green	Light true green, true green, emerald green, icy green	Blue-greens, pastel to deep	Grayed yellow-greens, yellow-greens lime to bright, earth greens (olive, moss, jade, forest)	Clear yellow-greens, pastel to bright
Orange	No orange	No orange	All oranges, deep peach, salmon, rust, terra cotta	Light oranges, apricot, peach, salmon, all corals, light rust
Pink	Shocking pink, deep hot pink (blue), magenta, fuchsia, icy pink	All pastel pinks (blue), deep rose, blue pinks	No pink	All peachy (yellow) pinks
Red	True red, blue-red	Watermelon, blue-reds, raspberry	Orange-reds, bittersweet dark tomato	Clear red, orange-reds
Burgundy	Bright burgundy	Burgundy, including maroons and cordovans	No burgundy	No burgundy
Gold	No gold	No gold	All golds	Clear gold
Yellow	Clear lemon yellow, icy yellow	Light lemon yellow	Yellow-gold	Bright golden yellow
Purple	Royal purple, icy violet	Plum, soft fuchsia, mauve, orchid, lavender	No purple	Medium violet, blue-violet

It is exciting to find out which season we are and what colors help us shine. But even more important is to have the person of Christ shine out of us because we have given Him daily access to our hearts. As we spend time with Him each day in His Word and in prayer, and as we keep our hearts listening to His voice and His leading, He will transform us so our inner beauty will shine in a way no external beauty can. This is because His Holy Spirit will be transforming our insides, and people will see more and more of Him in our attitudes and actions. His Spirit will be the focus, not our carnal nature. Ladies, this is what we want: to let His Spirit flow through us to others for His purposes and His glory. Let's allow Him to transform us into a beautiful fragrance for Him.

Lesson 7

Bonding

Esther's Difficult Situation

Read Esther 2:12–14.

1. What is this really describing?

2. How do you think Esther felt about going to the king for a one-night stand with no guarantee that she would become his queen?

3. Read the following two scriptures and write out a biblical view for dealing with difficult situations.

    a. Isaiah 55:8–9

    b. Romans 8:28

As we turn TO God, He uses every situation for our good.

Bonding

Do you know there is a bonding process that takes place in forming a proper marital bond that is tight and secure? These steps are listed in Dr. James Dobson's book *Love for a Lifetime*. They are a result of the research of Dr. Desmond Morris and the writings of Dr. Donald Joy. Joy and Morris maintain that a permanent bond or commitment is very likely to occur when couples move *systematically* and *slowly* through these twelve steps during their courtship and early marriage.[13] If these steps are not followed systematically and slowly, the result may not be a permanent bond or commitment.

The Twelve Steps of Bonding[14]

Read the description under each numbered step and then name the step next to the number. The last four steps are of a progressive, intimate nature and should be reserved for marriage. The gift of sex is from God. When reserved for marriage, it is a beautiful way to express the love and devotion of a husband and wife. It is the final cementing of the glue, bonding together a husband and wife.

1. *Eye to Body (first answer)*
   Observing other people will quickly allow you to assess many things about them: their physical build, sex, approximate age, possible social status, and perhaps something about their personality. These specifications will determine whether the other person is appealing.

2.

   When strangers of the opposite sex exchange glances, the natural reaction is to see each other and then quickly avert one's gaze. However, if both individuals look at each other and smile, it may mean they would like to get know each other better.

3.

   When conversing with others, we find out information. This may include their name, where they work, hobbies, opinions on topics, and more. If both people find they have many similar interests, they may become friends.

4.

   The first physical touch between two people is usually non-romantic. Many times it is simply the man helping a woman up or down, or across a difficult obstacle. If they have no more physical contact, the relationship usually remains platonic. Continuing to hold hands lets others know they are progressing beyond friendship.

5.

   Putting one's hand around the shoulder of the other person reveals a growing closeness in the relationship.

6.

   Putting one's hand around the waist of another pulls two people closer together. This allows feelings of closer intimacy to ensue.

7.

   Gazing into each other's eyes, hugging, and kissing are the next step toward forming a permanent bond. If the couple has not omitted the previous steps, they should have a good understanding of each other's nonverbal communication signals. At this time sexual desire is aroused in the couple.[15]

8.

As bonding continues, the couple will gradually start touching or stroking each other's hair or head while talking and kissing. This shows greater romantic attachment.

9.

Stroking or touching various parts of the body is primarily part of the foreplay to sexual acts. It should be reserved for marriage.

10.

Kissing the woman's breast. This is reserved for the expression of love and trust that has been built between a man and his wife. This also should be saved for marriage.

11.

Touching or stroking sexual organs as an expression of love, trust and passion between a husband and wife. This should be reserved for marriage.

12.

The ultimate sexual expression of love, trust and passion between a husband and wife.[16] This should be reserved for marriage.

Following these steps slowly and sequentially lays a good foundation for a safe and secure relationship.[17]

Oxytocin

Oxytocin is a bonding chemical God put in your body.[18] It is released in different amounts, depending on the type of stimulation. It is designed to create a bond between you and a potential husband.[19]

1. What would happen if you start having physical contact (even just hand holding) with someone to whom you are attracted, but he does not have your best interests at heart?

2. If you continued down the path of physical bonding with him, where could that potentially lead?

   a.

   b.

   c.

   d.

   e.

Two Different Relationships

During an interview on Focus on the Family, Dannah Gresh tells the story of a young woman and her relationships with two different men. Lady X had a five-year relationship with boyfriend A. They respected each other, had fun together, worked together, and had little physical contact. When they broke up, Lady X was sad but not devastated. She was able to move on with her life in a healthy way.[20]

Then came along boyfriend B. It was a short relationship—just a few months—but there was much more physical contact. Thus there was a lot more oxytocin put into her brain.[21]

1. How do you think lady X felt when she and boyfriend B broke up?

2. What was the difference in the relationship between boyfriend A and boyfriend B?

3. What did the difference in this physical contact cause?

Hooking-up

Today, we have a practice commonly called hooking up.[22] This is when a guy will have sex with a woman—any woman—for no real reason except to satisfy himself or brag to his friends.

1. What motivates a woman to hook up with a guy in the first place?

    a.

    b.

    c.

2. Because physical intimacy is when the most oxytocin is released into the brain, how do you think the woman feels when she leaves his bed in the morning or when they break up?

    a.

    b.

    c.

    d.

    e.

3. Did she get the affirmation that she desired?

Walk of Shame

"On college campuses, this morning-after walk is called the walk of shame. The name itself, walk of shame, shows that in the woman's heart, she knows something is very wrong."[23]

Watch how your boyfriend's father treats the members of his family, because that will be where your prospective husband learned his values and behavioral patterns. Look for his values and behavioral patterns before you start any physical contact.

If you have already gone further in your interaction with the opposite sex than you should have, please know that God still loves you and will forgive you. You need to come clean with Him by confessing your sins and asking for forgiveness. You also need to decide that you will refrain from that behavior and put up safety boundaries to help you succeed. These might include the following.

❖ Decide what physical contact you will have, and how much.
❖ Decide what physical contact you will not have until you are married.
❖ Never be alone with a guy in an apartment, hotel, or any other place where it is easy to fall into temptation.
❖ Limit the amount of time spent alone with a guy in a private setting. The less time alone, the less time to give into temptation.
❖ Do as many things as possible with a group or in a public setting.
❖ Be very selective about the type of guy with whom you hang out.

What other ideas do you have?

You may also want to get the help of a good Christian counselor or wise older woman to help you:

❖ work through the pain and confusion of what you have or are experiencing,
❖ discover why you went as far as you did,
❖ set appropriate boundaries for the future,
❖ discover the qualities to look for in a good mate, and
❖ have mentoring in future situations.

Values in a Husband or Good Friend

1. What are some values you would like in a husband or a very good friend?

    a.

    b.

    c.

    d.

    e.

    f.

    g.

    h.

2. What are some ways a man might show you that you are cherished?

    a.

    b.

c.

d.

e.

f.

g.

h.

i.

j.

k.

l.

m.

If the other person is emotionally healthy and you are emotionally healthy, then you can have a healthy relationship.

Esther: God's Provision

Read Esther 2:15–18.

    1.   Did Esther get to be the queen?

    2.   Was God taking care of her, even though at first it didn't seem like it?

    3.   Explain how God took care of Esther.

        a.

        b.

Esther's Example for Us

What should we do when life gets confusing and things seem out of control?

    1.

    2.

    3.

    4.

Lesson 8

Unfaltering Conviction

Mordecai Saves the King

Read Esther 2:19–23.

1. What was Mordecai's relationship to Esther (2:5–7)?

2. Where was he sitting (2:21)?

3. What was the significance of sitting in the king's gate?

> *"The gateway of ancient cities was its major commercial and legal center. Markets were held in gateways; the court sat there to transact its business. A king might even hold an audience there."*[24]

4. What did Mordecai hear (2:21)?

5. What did Mordecai do (2:22)?

6. What did Esther do (2:22)?

7. Then what happened (2:23)?

8. Was the incident forgotten (2:23)? Explain.

Mordecai Is Trustworthy

Let's look at one more detail in Esther 2:20.

1. Had Esther told anyone she was a Jew?

2. Why not?

3. Was this an angry obedience, or a trusting obedience?

4. Why do you think this? Support your answer.

Mordecai's love for Esther is a picture of Christ's love for us.

"For I know the plans I have for you, says the Lord, plans for welfare and not for evil, to give you a future and a hope." (Jeremiah 29:11)

Haman

Read Esther 3:1–6.

1. Who was promoted (3:1)?

2. Who was Haman (3:1)?

God or False Gods

1. Who was Mordecai (2:5–7, 21)?

    a.

    b.

    c.

2. Why did Mordecai's Jewish heritage keep him from bowing to Haman?

3. Read Exodus 20:3–5a.
    a. What do we learn from this scripture?

    b. What are some of the graven images or "gods" that we currently have in our lives? List them in the squares.

Table 6: Current "gods."

1	5	9
2	6	10
3	7	11
4	8	12

   c. How do we know when they have become our "god" or idol?

      1)

      2)

      3)

      4)

   d. If we find we have made something an idol, what should we do?

      1)

      2)

      3)

      4)

Haman versus Mordecai

1. What was Haman's reaction when it was pointed out to him that Mordecai would not bow down to him (3:5)?

2. Why?

3. What did he plan to do because of his injured pride (3:6)?

4. Why kill all the Jews (3:6)?

5. What was Haman's motive?

Dealing with Injustice

1. Have you ever had your pride hurt by untrue accusations?

2. How did you feel?

3. Did you want to get revenge?

4. Read Romans 12:17–21. List the things God tells us to do in this passage.

   a.

   b.

c.

d.

e.

f.

g.

5. Why are we to be kind to our enemy?

    a.

    b.

6. Why are we to leave vengeance, or punishment of the crime, to God?

    a.

    b.

    c.

7. Read Matthew 5:23–24. What should we do when we have offended someone?

This is how strongly God wants relationships restored.

Before attempting to be reconciled to another, it is wise to spend time with God and do following. (The leader will help you finalize this list.)

a.

b.

c.

d.

e.

8. Read Matthew 18:15–17, Matthew 5:44, and Matthew 10:16. List the steps we are to take when a Christian sins against us.

a.

b.

c.

d.

e.

f.

Forgiving and reconciling are two different things. Forgiving is giving up our right to get even and releasing our ill feelings. Reconciling is restoring the relationship to one based on truth and trust.

As Christians, we need to know how to handle conflict God's way and do what God teaches. If we do, our conscience will be at peace.

Mordecai Walked in Obedience to God, Despite Opposition

What did Mordecai risk in order to live in obedience to God, bowing only to Him and not to man?

1.

2.

3.

4.

Mordecai's Steps in Handling a Big Problem

1. How did Mordecai handle this problem? Write what you learn from these scriptures.

    a. Esther 4:1–2

    b. Esther 4:8

c. Esther 4:13–14

d. Esther 4:15–16

e. Esther 4:15–17

f. Esther 4:17

2. What does Mordecai's response to Haman's edict show us about our emotions?

God created our emotions. It is fine to express them in an appropriate manner that hurts no one. However, we shouldn't stay there.

❖ *We need to turn to God for His direction, because He is the only One who can help us. He can orchestrate circumstances for our deliverance.*
❖ *We should enlist the prayer support of others.*
❖ *Under God's direction, we may need to ask others for help.*
❖ *We need to continue to walk in obedience to God.*
❖ *We need to trust Him with the outcome.*

Mordecai did all these things. We never hear of him bowing to Haman. He followed God with unfaltering conviction when it would have been much easier to bow to Haman. Instead, he chose to honor God and do things His way. This is what we need to do also. We need to seek God, walk in obedience to Him, and trust Him for the outcome. The results of our obedience may bring hardship or difficulty for a short or long period of time, but we need to trust Him. We need to realize that He is God, not people. He will take us through the storms of this life. If we keep trusting Him and walking in obedience to Him, He will guide us through this life and safely into heaven for eternity.

Lesson 9

Haman's Plot against the Jews

Last week, we saw the plot thicken as Haman found out that Mordecai was a Jew, and so he determined to kill not only Mordecai but also all the Jews.

Haman's Empowerment

Read Esther 3:7–11.

1. What did Haman ask the king to do (3:8–9)?

2. What did the king give Haman to show his support of Haman's request (3:10)?

3. Why was it important for Haman to have the king's signet ring?

Passover

1. During which month did Haman begin his plot to destroy the Jews (3:7)?

2. What is significant about this month (Exodus 12:1-11)?

3. What is Passover? Read Exodus 12:1–36 and write down what you discover.

*As Israel was delivered from the bondage of slavery to the nation of Egypt, so
we are delivered from our bondage to sin and forgiven of our past sins.*

*Being delivered from our bondage to sin does not mean we will never
sin again. It means sin no longer has power over us!*

*As we want to celebrate our deliverance from sin and live a victorious
life, Satan and his allies work to bring us back into bondage.*

Biblical Principles Concerning Sin and Temptation

Let's read several scriptures outside of Esther looking for some biblical principles that will help us understand sin and temptation. These will help us be aware of some of the ways that both God and Satan work. This knowledge can keep us from succumbing to Satan's schemes to take us back into bondage, and it can help us be victorious through seeking God.

1. Read Genesis 2:16–17 and Joshua 24:15. What do we learn from these two scriptures?

    a.

    b.

    c.

2. Read James 1:13–15. What truths do we learn concerning sin and temptation?

    a.

    b.

    c.

d.

e.

3. Using Genesis 2:16–17, Joshua 24:15, and James 1:13–15, list eight biblical principles concerning sin and temptation. (Combine all the answers from questions 1 and 2.)

   a.

   b.

   c.

   d.

   e.

   f.

   g.

   h.

   God does not make other people do wrong things to us; they do it by their own free will. Thus, we cannot blame God for their wrong actions.

Progressive Steps into Sin

Using James 1:14–15, list the progressive steps into sin.

1.

2.

3.

4.

5.

Satan's Strategies for Our Bondage

Jesus came to set us free from bondage to sin. Satan doesn't want us free. Instead, he and his allies work to bring us back into bondage.

1. Read Genesis 3:1–5. Using this passage, describe two ways Satan tries to bring us back into bondage.

   a.

      1) What are the three ways Satan lied in this passage?

         a)

         b)

      c)

    b.

God may not give us what we want because He may be protecting us from something we cannot handle maturely.

God's Goal for Our Lives

   1. Look up James 1:2–4. What is God's goal for our lives?

   2. Read James 1:16–17. What kind of gifts does God give us?

   3. Read Romans 8:28. How should we view a gift that looks bad?

Biblical Principles for Dealing with Our Pain and Hurt

Using the following scriptures, explain these biblical principles for dealing with some of the hurt and pain we have in this world.

   1. John 16:33b

   2. James 1:2–5, 13–14

   3. Romans 8:28; James 1:2–4, 17

   4.   James 1:17; Romans 8:28; John 16:33b; Joshua 24:15

A Third Strategy of Satan for Our Bondage

Read 1 Timothy 6:10. What is another way Satan tries to move us away from God and back into bondage?

> *Check your heart to see what is motivating you, what disappoints you, and what your goals are.*
>
> *"We were made for God and until He is our greatest pleasure, all the other pleasures of this life will lead to emptiness."*[25]

Haman's Deceitfulness

Read Esther 3:8–9.

   1.   Did Haman tell the truth concerning why he wanted the Jews killed?

   2.   What did he omit?

      a.

      b.

      c.

d.

3. What did Haman appeal to within the king that nudged him toward deciding in Haman's favor?

Guidelines for Making Good Decisions

As godly ladies we want to make good and wise decisions like Esther did. This will help everyone involved in the decision we are making concerning a specific issue. What lessons can we learn from Haman's deceitfulness and the king's blind trust that will help us make good decisions?

1.

2.

3.

4.

5.

6.

Results of an Unwise Decision

There were four responses to the king's decision and letter stating that the Jews were to be annihilated on the thirteenth day of Adar. The resulting confusion and fear illustrate how important it is to make wise decisions. Read Esther 3:13–15 and Esther 4:1–4 to discover these various responses.

1. What did the king and Haman do after the letter was sent out stating that the Jews were to be annihilated on the thirteenth day of Adar?

2. How did the people in the city react?

3. What was Mordecai's response to the letter?

4. How did the Jews throughout the entire empire respond?

God and Emotions

Look up the following passages and find out if God wants us to be honest about our feelings, and yet reach out to Him for help.

1. Matthew 11:28–29

2. 1 Peter 5:7

3. Isaiah 35:4

4. Isaiah 55:1–3

a. Do these scriptures reveal a God who doesn't care, or a God who cares greatly and understands our fears and needs?

b. What does God ask us to do in the middle of our fears and problems?

c. What does God say He will do?

Results of Turning to God

What happens within us when we turn to God with a problem, and He helps us?

1.

2.

3.

4.

5.

As we spend time with Him and trust Him, He gives us joy and fulfillment for the journey through life!

Lesson 10

Esther's Choice

Have you ever had a time when you had to make a difficult choice between two different directions for your life? If you chose A, your life would take a particular course. If you chose B, your life would go in a different direction.

We will start in the fourth chapter of Esther and see what dilemma Esther had, as well as the choice she made.

Esther's Problem

Read Esther 4:1–4.

1. What was Mordecai doing (4:1–4)?

2. When Esther heard that her uncle was mourning, what did she do (4:4)?

3. Why do you think she did that?

4. Was her gift of clothing going to solve the problem or take away his distress?

5. Why didn't her gift of clothing solve the problem or take away his distress?

6. Does ignoring a problem, pretending it isn't there, putting salve on it, or walking away resolve the problem?

Keys to Solving Problems

There are several keys to having God help us with our problems. Let's look up some scriptures and discover them.

1. Read John 8:31–32. What is the first key in dealing with problems?

2. Read John 14:6. Who is Truth?

   a. Why do we need to know Jesus in order to effectively deal with our issues?

   b. How can we know Jesus (Truth)?

   c. He tells us if we "continue in His word" (John 8:31-32), we will be His disciples, know Him, and be set free. What does "continue in His word" mean?

   d. What are two things we can do to continue in His word?

      1)

      2)

> *If we listen and walk with Him, He will reveal to us:*
> ❖ *truths we need to know,*
> ❖ *bondages in our own lives and how to overcome them, and*
> ❖ *how to deal with problems and difficult people.*

Once we deal with a particular problem, we will be free in that area. When we are free inside, then we are free indeed! We are no longer bogged down internally with that issue!

Scriptural Guidelines for Solving Problems

1. Read 1 Peter 5:7 and James 1:5 to find out how God wants us to deal with our problems.

    a. Using these two scriptures, what two steps should we take when encountering a problem?

        1)

        2)

    b. Does God say He will give us the wisdom we need to deal with the problem?

    c. What do we have to do to get His wisdom?

        1)

        2)

2. Read Matthew 7:24–27.

    a. Who is the foolish person?

    b. Who is the wise person?

    This is the most critical part of our walk with God: to walk with Him in a relationship of love and obedience, seeking Him, listening, and doing what He says. It's not always easy, but when you get through each issue, it brings freedom, joy, and a wonderful feeling of God's love and presence.

3. We have gone through several concepts involved in solving a problem. List the steps to take when you have a problem.

   a.

   b.

   c.

   d.

   e.

   f.

Esther's Steps in Handling Her Problem

1. Read Esther 4:4–5.

   a. In review, what was Esther's first response to the problem?

   b. What was her second response?

   c. Could she talk directly to Mordecai?

   d. What did she do to communicate with him?

If we have a relationship with God, He will speak to our hearts through the scripture and His Holy Spirit.

2. Read Esther 4:6–9.

    a. What happened here?

    b. What did Mordecai ask Esther to do (4:8)?

3. Read Esther 4:10–11. What message did Esther send to Mordecai?

4. Read Esther 4:13–14.
    a. Mordecai told Esther two things and issued her a challenge. What were the two things he told her?

        1)

        2)

    b. What challenge did he give her to consider (4:14)?

        Maybe God has put you there for a reason!

        Allow yourself to be God's servant!

5. Read Esther 4:15–17.

    a. Did Esther agree to go to the king?

b. What was Esther's condition for doing as Mordecai asked?

c. Esther went through a number of steps before she was willing to consider going to the king. What were the first three steps Esther took in trying to solve her problem?

   1)

   2)

   3)

d. Did she do as he instructed without thinking?

e. What did she do?

f. Did she close her heart to more input?

g. How do we know that?

h. What were the next steps Esther took after receiving the original instruction that she should go to the king and beg for their lives?

   1)

   2)

   3)

4)

5)

     Queen Esther was sold out to God. When we are willing to find out God's will and then do it—because we are His servants, regardless of the outcome or consequences—then we are vessels of honor for our Lord.

Lesson 11

Esther's Intervention

Today, we are going to read about Esther going to the king. Remember that because she had not been summoned, she could die just for going to him.

Esther's Source of Power

Read Esther 5:1. How many days had it been since Esther had asked Mordecai to gather the Jews to fast and pray while she and her maids did the same?

Esther was prayed up. She was going in the strength and power of God, not in her own strength and wisdom. Ladies, this is what we need to do every day: spend time daily with God, seek Him, listen, and then walk in His wisdom and strength.

Esther Approaches the King

Read Esther 5:1–5.

1. Did Esther barge into the palace and go right up to the king?

2. What did she do?

3. What did the king do (5:2)?

4. Why did the king do this (5:2)?

5. Read the following two scriptures to discern why Esther may have found favor with the king.

   a. Ezra 6:22

   b. Esther 5:1

6. Read the following two scriptures to try to discover what might have caused the king to hold out his scepter to Esther.

   a. Esther 5:1

   b. Esther 5:1–2

Esther's Request

1. What did Esther request (5:4)?

2. Why did she do that?

3. Read Esther 5:6–8 and list two events that happened at the banquet.

   a.

   b.

Esther's Steps in Dealing with Her Problem

What steps did Esther take that we might use when dealing with an issue?

1.

2.

3.

4.

5.

6.

Lesson 12

Haman's Source of Self-worth

This week we will be discussing self-worth (or internal value) and forgiveness. When we feel we have value within ourselves, it is easier to see the value in others and forgive them. Forgiveness is a difficult process. We will discuss it after looking at our own internal value. Let's resume the study, looking at the two topics of self-worth and forgiveness.

Last week, Esther went to the king and invited him and Haman to a banquet. At this point, the banquet has ended, and she has invited them to another one. Let's pick up the story there.

Our Moods: Determined by Trust in God or by Situations?

Read Esther 5:9–14.

1. How did Haman respond to Esther's request for him to attend a second banquet (5:9)?

2. What turned his joy to anger (3:5; 5:9)?

3. Is letting situations determine our mood a mature response?

4. What should determine our moods?

5. How can we get a joyful outlook on life when something upsetting happens? Read the following scriptures and write down what you learn.

    a. Psalm 18:6a

    b. 1 Peter 5:7

    c. Psalm 34:4

    d. Psalm 86:11

    e. Psalm 56:3

    f. 2 Corinthians 10:5

    g. Psalm 123:1–2

6. What was the real source of Haman's anger?

When we are angry or upset, we should ask God to help us look into our hearts and reveal the real root of our feelings. Is it anger, pain, rejection, bitterness, fear, jealousy, or control? What is it? In order to find freedom, we need to:

a.

b.

Haman's Source of Value

1. What did Haman do to make himself feel better after seeing the "non-bowing" Mordecai (5:10–12)?

2. Did that change the situation?

3. Did his assets, power, and position really make him someone of value?

4. Besides bragging, how else did he try and retain his sense of self-worth?

5. Can we really control other people or circumstances?

6. Are external sources or controlling people and situations a good foundation from which to form a good self-image?

Haman had some very unstable sources for determining his self-worth. His self-image was determined by his assets, sons, position, and power, as well as how well he could control people and situations. If these crumbled, then so did his self-worth.

The World's Source of Value

1. What criteria does the world use to determine a person's value?

    a.

    b.

    c.

    d.

    e.

    f.

    g.

2. If our value is based on these things, for how long do we have value?

3. Let's say there is a beautiful actress whose claim to fame is her good looks. She gets in a car wreck, and her face and body are disfigured. Does she suddenly lose her value? Explain why or why not.

> *Although God didn't cause the car wreck, He may offer her a greater purpose than simply being an actress and serving herself.*
>
> *Surrendering our hurts, bitterness, and anger to God can change our lives. It can have a positive rippling effect on the lives of others.*

The True and Lasting Source of Value

1. Read Matthew 6:26. Jesus shared two truths in this verse. What are they?

    a.

b.

2. Read Genesis 1:26–28. After whose image were you created?

3. What does it mean to be created in God's image?

Being God's loved and cherished creation gives us immense value.

God Loves Us

God gave us guidelines in His book to protect us from things that will hurt and harm us. He doesn't give us guidelines to stop our fun. He gives us guidelines because He loves us and doesn't want us hurt. He wants what is best for us.

1. Read Matthew 7:11. What do you learn from this verse?

2. Read 2 Chronicles 16:9a. Who may enjoy the benefits of God's blessings?

God knows we will not be perfect, but we need to try to keep our hearts (our motives) right before Him. Spend time with God daily and ask Him to help you do a regular "heart check."

If your heart is not at peace, what are some "heart check" things you can do to regain your peace? (The leader will help supply this list.)

a.

b.

c.

d.

e.

f.

Haman's Way of Dealing with Life

Read Esther 5:12–14.

1. Did Haman's assets—his position, fame, money, friends, family, and more—bring him contentment?

2. How did Haman's wife and friends suggest he deal with Mordecai (5:14)?

3. How were they telling Haman to solve his problem?

A Biblical Viewpoint on Dealing with Difficulties

1. Read Matthew 5:44. Does God advise us to get rid of people who irritate us?

2. Read the following two scriptures and explain why God might allow people into our lives who irritate us.

    a.   Hebrews 12:10

    b.   Proverbs 27:17

> *God can use irritating people and circumstances that are difficult to help conform us into His image.*
>
> *God uses the circumstances of our lives to purify us and skim off the dross, until what is seen in us is His image.*
>
> *Through the power of His Spirit, we can be healed.*

Forgiveness

1.   Discuss how you can forgive someone who has hurt you deeply, and perhaps repeatedly.

2.   List some steps to take in working toward forgiveness and reconciliation. (The leader will supplement this list.)

    a.

    b.

    c.

    d.

e.

f.

g.

h.

i.

j.

3. Let's read through some scriptures, seeking to understand this list on forgiveness and reconciliation.
   a. Read Matthew 18:23–35.
      1) Who does the king represent?

      2) Who do the servants represent?

      3) How much money did the king forgive the first servant (18:24–27)?

      4) What was the amount of money the first servant refused to forgive the second servant (18:28–30)?

      5) What is the extent of God's forgiveness toward us?

6) How much do you forgive compared to God's forgiveness?

7) What does God want of us?

b. Read Matthew 6:14–15. What do you learn from this scripture?

God is saying, "I have forgiven you so much! Can't you forgive your fellow human out of gratitude for the forgiveness I have freely given you?" Yet forgiveness is not easy.

4. What is forgiveness?

Picture yourself laying the offending person, the pain, and the bitterness at the feet of Jesus or at the foot of the cross. Say that you forgive it, and then leave it there. Sometimes you may need to lay it down again many times, especially if it was very painful.

When you feel anger or bitterness, then you know you are having trouble forgiving. Discover what it is and lay it at the feet of Jesus.

If you are still having trouble forgiving completely, you may need to picture that "root of bitterness" (Hebrews 12:15) like the roots of a tree going down into your body from your mouth. It might be helpful to sit down and ask God to help you keep pulling all the roots out through your mouth, even the tiny "hair roots," until all those roots are out. Then, you will finally be free!

There may have been some things so painful in your life that you do not want to forgive. God understands and knows. Because we know He wants us to forgive, we can pray, "Lord, I do not want to forgive that person. My heart is hard with pain. You are going to have to help me get to the point where I will be willing to give You permission to help me even think about forgiving them."

If we sincerely pray that prayer, pretty soon God will begin to work in our hearts. He will lead us to the point that we can give Him permission to help us begin to think about starting the forgiving process.

Forgiveness Differs from Reconciliation

1. Is forgiveness the same as reconciliation or restoring the relationship?

2. What is the difference?

3. Does God want us to reconcile with everyone we have forgiven?
   a. Read Romans 12:18.
   b. What can we learn from this passage?

4. Why might it not be possible to live peaceably with everyone?

5. What determines whether you can restore a relationship?

This means both parties must be truthful. Genuine confession of a specific sin (or sins) is made with a request for forgiveness. Then the process of trust must be rebuilt with consistent, trustable behavior in a safe environment. If unsafe behavior resurfaces, then the relationship may need to be severed again until there is true repentance and a new pattern of safe behavior is established. Some people never will repent or behave in a way that is safe for you to reconcile with them.

6. Read Mark 12:28–31. What does Jesus say are the two most important commandments?
   a.

b.

1) If you are an emotionally healthy person, would you intentionally hurt yourself?

2) If you are in a relationship with someone who intentionally and repeatedly hurts you, is he or she a safe person with whom to maintain a relationship?

If you are in a relationship with someone who intentionally and repeatedly hurts you, that person does not really love you and is unsafe. Love yourself enough to protect yourself and get out of the relationship.

If you are absolutely certain God is calling you to show His agape love to someone with whom you have a difficult relationship, then proceed as God directs.

However, God may be leading you to a safer place. This may involve leading you out of this relationship until the other person is willing to become healthy.

Seek God's direction!

God does want us to forgive and, if possible, reconcile with everyone. He knows it may not be possible to reconcile with everyone. But we can forgive! And oh, the freedom and release when we do forgive someone and release them to God!

I want you to know that with God, forgiving and healing is possible. He wants to and is able to heal you! Isn't that wonderful?

Isn't it exciting to be in the process of becoming the beautiful woman of God that He envisions in each one of us? The more we are freed from the "dross," and the more the chains of fear, rejection, anger, pain, workaholic tendencies, perfectionism, and lack of forgiveness fall off, the freer we are on the inside. Then we are freer to love and enjoy God, life, and other people. God wants us internally free and whole!

John 8:36 says, "So if the Son makes you free, you will be free indeed."

Let God set you free! It's a process, but let Him set you free!

Lesson 13

Coincidence or Divine Intervention?

Last week, Haman's friends and wife advised him to get rid of his irritation (Mordecai) by building a gallows fifty cubits (approximately seventy-five feet) high on which to hang Mordecai. Let's continue with the story.

A Sleepless Night

Read Esther 6:1–11.

1. Esther 6:1 reveals that the king could not sleep that night. Why do you think he couldn't sleep?

   a. Read Proverbs 21:1. What can we learn from this scripture?

   b. With this scripture in mind, why might the king not have been able to sleep?

2. What did the king ask for (6:1)?

3. What did the king "just happen" to read in the book (6:2)?

4. How did the king feel toward Mordecai after reading that he had saved his life (6:3)?

5. What request did Haman desire to ask of the king (6:4)?

6. Would the king feel like hanging Mordecai after finding out he had saved his life?

7. Who orchestrated the king's inability to sleep and his reading of Mordecai's saving act?

God Takes Care of His People

1. Read 1 Samuel 2:9. What three things do we learn from this scripture?

    a.

    b.

    c.

2. Who took care of Mordecai and Esther in this situation?

    God orchestrated the redeeming circumstances, and He can do the same in each of our lives—if we turn to Him, seek His direction and assistance, do as He directs, watch Him work, and realize our deliverance is from Him.

Haman's Humiliation

1. What did the king have Haman do to honor Mordecai (6:7–11)?

2. Who suggested this way to honor Mordecai (6:6–9)?

3. Why did he suggest it (6:6)?

4. What did wearing the royal robes, a king's crown, etc., signify?

Attaining Worldly Significance Does Not Satisfy

1. Does power or a high position bring significance, meaning and purpose to a person's life?

*Augustine famously wrote, "Thou hast made us for Thyself, O Lord,
and our heart is restless until it finds its rest in Thee."*[26]

2. Read James 4:1–4.
   a. Why do we wound and hurt other people?

   b. Rather than hurting others, what three things does James tell us to do?

      1)

      2)

      3)

> *That is what Mordecai and Esther did.*
> ❖ *They humbled themselves before God.*
> ❖ *They were afraid and turned to God in prayer and fasting.*
> ❖ *They sought to do God's will and save the lives of the Jews.*
> ❖ *God acted on their behalf, and He even had Mordecai honored.*

Pride Goes Before a Fall

Read Esther 6:12–14.

1. What was Haman's emotional response after the king had Mordecai honored (6:12)?

2. Why do you think he covered his head?

3. What did his family say (6:13)?

4. Haman's pride was revealed by his great desire to be honored and to have a position of power. Read Proverbs 16:5, Proverbs 16:18, and Proverbs 21:4 to discover God's view of pride. Why do you think pride is a sin?

   a. Read 1 Peter 5:6.

   b. What can we learn from Proverbs 16:5, Proverbs 16:18, Proverbs 21:4, and 1 Peter 5:6?

      1)

      2)

      3)

4)

5. What was Haman's emotional state when he went to dine with Queen Esther the second time (Esther 6:12–14)?

6. Why was Haman upset?

7. In what emotional state had he planned to go to the queen's banquet (5:9–12)?

8. What was giving Haman a sense of security and pride?

9. Will any of these things last forever and therefore be a source of real security?

Our Security Should Be in God

Read the following scriptures to discover the One in whom it is safe to place our trust.

1. Read John 2:24–25.

   a. Why didn't Jesus trust men?

   b. Have you experienced people turning on you? One day they are your friend, and the next they're your enemy. How did that make you feel?

   c. If people are fickle, and if possessions, wealth, and physical appearance do not last, where should our trust be?

2. Read Psalm 37:39–40.

    a. What do we learn about God from this Psalm?

    b. Whom does He help?

    c. Read Romans 6:12–13, Romans 13:13–14, and Galatians 3:27. Describe "the righteous."

3. Read John 14:15. How do we show God we love Him?

4. Read Psalm 37:39-40. If we are walking in a right relationship with God, what will He do?

    a. Does God have the power to help us?

    b. Does man have the power to help us?

    c. Where should we place our trust?

When Encountering Problems, Seek God's Help and Direction

1. Read Esther 4:15–17. When God asks us to trust Him, does He want us to sit around doing nothing?

    a. What did Mordecai and Esther do?

b. What was the purpose of fasting? (For an example, you may read 2 Chronicles 20:1–4.)

c. What is the first thing we should do when we encounter problems?

2. Read 1 Samuel 30:1–10, 18–19 to discover how David handled a difficult problem.

3. God's answer will be specific for each situation. What should we do when God says nothing?[27] (The leader will assist with these answers.)

    a.

    b.

    c.

4. After seeking God and getting His direction, what should you do?

    a. Read 1 Samuel 15:1–3, 10–23. (The approximate date of this story is 1025 BC.[28] Thus, it took place about 565 years before the story of Esther. This sad story in Saul's life shows us that there are consequences to disobeying God.)

    b. What did Samuel the prophet tell Saul (1 Samuel 15:22–23)?

God Guides His People in Various Ways

If we are His children and are sincerely seeking Him, His Holy Spirit will lead us in at least four different ways.[29]

Read the following scriptures and write down some ways God may lead His people.

1. 2 Timothy 3:16–17

2. Acts 16:6–10

3. Matthew 7:7–8; John 10:27

4. Acts 21:7–14

Steps for Solving Problems

1. Using the concepts learned in this lesson, list the steps we should take when encountering a problem.

    a.

    b.

    c.

    d.

    e.

2. Did Esther turn to God?

3. Did she wait for His direction?

Be sensitive in your heart to the leading of His Spirit. Even if you do not understand, follow His leading. He knows the big picture.

Lesson 14

Esther's Request

We now find Esther, the king, and Haman at the second banquet.

Esther Reveals the Plot for Her and Her People's Death

Read Esther 7:1–10.

1. When the king asks Esther what her petition is, how does she answer him?

2. When she says, "If I have found favor in your sight," what does this do to the king's emotions, and why?

3. When she says, "If it please the king, let my life be given me at my petition, and the life of my people at my request. For we are sold, I and my people, to be destroyed, to be slain, to be annihilated," what emotions do you think the king had?

4. Esther says (paraphrased), "If we were just sold as slaves, I would have said nothing. But our deaths and the affliction from that is nothing compared with the loss that will be for the king." What is she telling the king?

    a.

    b.

The Holy Spirit Empowers His People

How could Esther be so articulate?

1. Read Matthew 10:19–20. This is Jesus speaking to his disciples.

2. What do we learn from this scripture?

3. Let's turn to Acts 3 and Acts 4:1–4. The following is a summary.
    The time frame for this chapter was after the death and resurrection of Jesus. It was also after the empowering of the church by the Holy Spirit at Pentecost. Peter and John went to the temple and saw a man lame from birth. Peter healed the man, and that drew a crowd. When Peter started telling the crowd about Jesus, he and John were thrown into prison. In the morning, they were taken before the Sanhedrin, the supreme court of the Jews.

4. To continue the story, read Acts 4:5–13.
    a. Were Peter and John educated, articulate men?

    b. Read the following two scriptures and explain why Peter and John were bold and able to speak articulately.

        1) Acts 4:8

        2) Acts 4:13

Identity of the Holy Spirit

Read John 14:15–26.

1. Who is the Holy Spirit?

2. What do we call H_2O?

We see God in three forms: Father, Son, and Spirit. These all look different to us, and each one performs some different and unique function, yet they are one in essence.

3. Read John 14:15–17. What do we need to do in order to have the Holy Spirit reside in us and help us?

4. In John 14:15–26, what are the names given to the Holy Spirit?

   a. John 14:16

      1) What do you think of when you hear the word *counselor*?

   b. John 14:17

      1) What do you think of when you hear *Spirit of Truth*?

         a) Spirit

         b) Truth

   c. John 14:26

      1) What do you think of when you hear these two terms?

         a) Counselor

         b) Holy Spirit

What Does the Holy Spirit Do?

Using John 14:15–27, list seven things that Jesus says the Holy Spirit will do.

1. John 14:16

2. John 14:17

3. John 14:21

4. John 14:23

5. John 14:26

6. John 14:26

7. John 14:27

> *These are wonderful truths for us concerning the Holy Spirit! We simply need to be listening and walking in obedience so He can help us.*

Esther Reveals Haman as the Enemy

1. How does the king respond to Esther's revelation concerning her impending death (7:5)?

2. What does the king do when he hears this news (7:7)?

3. What do you think he's doing after he leaves them?

4. What does Haman do when Esther boldly accuses him of his wicked deed (7:7–8)?

5. What does the king say when he sees Haman on the queen's couch (7:8)?

When your only source of strength is yourself and you don't trust in God, you can do some pretty desperate things.

Haman's Demise

1. Who suggested to the king that Haman be hanged (7:9)?

2. What happened to Haman (7:10)?

3. Read Proverbs 29:23 and Proverbs 16:18.
    a. What had Haman done in his heart?

    b. What other wicked deed was he planning to do?

    c. What was the result?

A Christ-like Response When We Have Been Wronged

1. What should we do when someone else gets a position or receives the recognition we feel is due us?

2. Think back over the lessons that we have had. What steps should we take if we are being wronged?

   a.

   b.

   c.

   d.

   e.

   f.

   g.

Second Half of Lesson

The information for the following section is found in *Color Me Beautiful's Looking Your Best* by Mary Spillane and Christine Sherlock.[30]

God created a variety of body types, and each one if beautiful! Let's discover them – and which body type you have.

Various Body Types[31]

1. Inverted Triangle: The shoulders are wider than the hips.
2. Straight: Hip and shoulder measurements are fairly even.
3. Softened Straight: Hip and shoulder measurements are even, with a more defined waist.
4. Angular Pear: A straight or lean body, with the hips wider than the shoulders.
5. Curved Pear: The hips and thighs are larger than the shoulders.
6. Hourglass: The bust and hips are larger with a narrow waist.
7. Round: Most of the weight in the bust, waist, and thighs.

People may also be long- or short-waisted, or have a uniform torso.[32]

1. Short-waisted: You have a short waist but may have long legs.
2. Long-waisted: You may have lots of room for belts but have short legs.
3. Uniform torso: Your waist is equal distance between the armpit and the crotch. Your crotch is equal distance between the head and feet, and your knee is halfway down the leg.[33]

Tips for Non-uniform Torsos [34]

1. Short-waisted
   a. Select narrow belts and tone them with the color of your outfit.
   b. Avoid short, cropped, bolero-style jackets. A longer jacket will help balance your look.
   c. If you have great legs, shorter skirts look wonderful.
   d. If you're long-legged, draw attention from your short waist to your legs.

2. Long-waisted
   a. Short jackets can bring attention to the waist.
   b. Choose wide, colorful belts, or match them to the bottom of your ensemble, giving the illusion of longer legs.
   c. Pair a long jacket with a short skirt just slightly longer than the jacket.

3. Short Legs/Long Torso
   a. Create attention at or above the waist with belts.
   b. Short to hip-length jackets are best.
   c. To lengthen short legs, wear shorter skirts and hosiery toned with your skirt and shoes.

4. Long Legs/Short Torso
   a. Long hemlines, detailed hemlines, and various kinds of pleats look great on long legs.
   b. Keep shorter hemlines just above the knee.
   c. Avoid high-heeled shoes because they appear to lengthen the leg.
   d. Use interesting hosiery to draw attention to longer legs.
   e. Wear longer jackets (to mid-thigh) and small belts.
   f. Long-waisted dresses, over-blouses, long sweaters, and low-slung belts help create the illusion of balanced proportions.

How to Dress the Various Body Types[35]

1. Inverted Triangle Shape
   a. Characteristics: Two Types
      1) Boyish or athletic.
      2) Broad-shouldered, larger busted, flat-bottomed women.
   b. Wear sharp, crisp styles, rather than flowing, soft fashions.
   c. Don't accentuate shoulders with pads.
   d. If full busted, keep details in that area minimal.
   e. Wear tightly woven fabrics in your blouses and jackets to make you look smaller on top and balanced with your smaller lower half.
   f. Simple designs, rather than fussy prints, make for a dramatic statement.
   g. Gathers at the waist can make you look heavy.
   h. Show off your legs with short-length skirts or interesting details in your hem (kick-pleats, gored skirts, contrasting trim).
   i. A low heel or flat shoe helps balance your body type.
   j. Examples: Princess Stephanie of Monaco and the model Iman.

2. Straight Body Type
   a. Characteristics: Shoulders and hips almost in a line, and the waist not more than six inches less than the hips.
   b. Wear tightly woven fabrics.
   c. Wear sharply structured or unstructured designs.
   d. Jackets and dresses that contour a little at the waist are good.
   e. Keep attention to the waist minimal.
   f. Waistlines on skirts and slacks should have minimal (if any) gathers.
   g. Sleeves should be straight, tapered, and crisp.
   h. Set-in sleeves are best.
   i. Examples: Nancy Reagan and Princess Diana.

3. The Softened Straight Shape
   a. Characteristics: The same straight shoulder line, but a more defined waist.
   b. Wear tightly woven fabrics.
   c. Belts are a great accessory.
   d. Inverted pleats and soft gathers used in moderation are best.
   e. Tight to moderate weaves are best at showing off your good lines.
   f. Use simple styles with little volume and definition at the waist.
   g. Fitted jackets look best, but a loose jacket that is belted or left open to show off the waist is good.
   h. Examples: Princess Caroline of Monaco and Meryl Streep.

4. The Angular Pear Shape
    a. Characteristics: Narrow at the shoulders and broadest through the hips with larger flat thighs, a flat tummy, and flat hips.
    b. Key: Broaden the shoulders with straight shoulder pads to balance the hips.
    c. Create a widening shoulder effect by wearing puffed or pleated sleeves, or peaked or pointed lapels on jackets. Drape shawls or scarves over the shoulders.
    d. Tightly woven fabric with simple designs and without excessive flounces or gathers looks best.
    e. Larger jackets that aren't too big can provide balance.
    f. Layering above the waist creates volume and balance for your frame.
    g. Example: Hillary Clinton.

5. The Curved Pear Shape
    a. Characteristics: Smaller on the top and broader through the hips, with a curvy silhouette from the front and sides.
    b. Avoid slim fitting tops. Add layers and volume above the waist with scarves and shawls to balance your figure.
    c. Boat necklines create a widening illusion, and draping crossover necklines add softness and compliment your figure.
    d. Use soft pleats and gathers at the waist, but not completely around the waist, because it will make you look larger.
    e. Fabrics should be soft and loosely woven; a crisp fabric will make you look heavier.
    f. Patterns should be soft: florals, curved abstracts, paisleys.
    g. Example: Oprah Winfrey.

6. The Hourglass Shape
    a. Characteristics: A soft shoulder line, with curves from front and side profiles.
    b. The waist is defined, the hips are rounded, and the bottom and bust are pronounced (but not necessarily large).
    c. It's difficult to find professional suits or dresses for this body type.
    d. Select soft fabrics in florals, polka dots, and paisleys.
    e. Designs need to be soft, gathered, and eased, with soft pleats.
    f. Necklines are draped, round, crossover, or ruffled.
    g. Baggy, loose tops will make you look frumpy or larger than you are.
    h. Lapels of jackets should not be sharp, but rounded.
    i. Accentuate the waist (which is at least ten inches smaller than the hips) with eased waistlines, not straight darts.
    j. Examples: Sophia Loren and Dolly Parton.

7. Round Body Shape
    a. Characteristics: Most of weight is in the tummy, hips, thighs, bust, and upper arms.
    b. Keep your look loose and unstructured, not tight.
    c. Keep attention on your face with soft collars, attractive necklaces, or scarves.
    d. Tops and dresses should drop in a simple, straight line from the shoulder.
    e. Avoid attention at the waistline, but ease fabric there with soft gathers.
    f. Too much draping, texture, fabric, or patterns can make you look heavier.
    g. Longer jackets, drop waistlines, and longer tunics can be slimming.
    h. Example: Roseanne Barr.

We don't have to have a specific body type to be beautiful.
Every body type is beautiful!

Lesson 15

What a Turn-around!

When we left Esther last week, she had just informed the king of Haman's evil plot. As a result, the king commanded that Haman be hung on the gallows he had made for Mordecai.

We are still at the palace with Esther and the king, after the exit of Haman.

Rewarded

Read Esther 8:1–2.

    1.   What did the king give Esther (8:1)?

    2.   What did Esther tell the king concerning Mordecai (8:1)?

        a.   How do you think the revelation that Mordecai had raised Esther and was her cousin made the king feel toward Mordecai?

        b.   Why?

    3.   When Mordecai came before the king, what did the king give him (8:2)?

    4.   Who had previously had his signet ring (3:10)?

5. What was the significance of the king giving Mordecai his ring (8:8)?

6. Because all was well with Esther and Mordecai, shouldn't they be happy and satisfied? Explain your answer.

Agape

Read Esther 8:3–17.

1. What did Esther do (8:3)?

   a. Using 1 Corinthians 13:4–7, John 15:12–13, and Hebrews 13:8, why did Esther beg for the life of her fellow Jews?

   b. In this world of "look out for number one," what does this story and God's word teach us about the value of looking out for the welfare of others?

Official Protection

1. What was the king's response to Esther's request to protect the Jews (Esther 8:8)?

2. How was an edict or letter sealed with the king's ring?

3. What did Mordecai write (8:10–11)?

4. When was this to happen (8:12)?

5. What was significant about that day (Esther 3:13)?

6. Who received copies of this letter (8:9)?

7. How did the Jews react to this edict (8:16–17)?

8. How did the Gentiles (non-Jews) react to the edict (8:17)?

9. What happened to Mordecai (8:15)?

Do Life God's Way

1. Why did this wonderful turn of events happen?

2. What did Mordecai and Esther do that opened the way for God to work with them and bring about the salvation of the Jews?

   a.

   b.

   c.

3. What should we do with our lives?

   a.

b.

c.

d.

God may not make you the hero or heroine, but He will help you, heal you, care for you, and love you perfectly. All He asks is for you to give your life to Him, walk in loving obedience, and trust Him.

Lesson 16

The Thirteenth Day of Adar

The story now fast-forwards to that fateful day of Adar.

The Thirteenth Day of Adar

Read Esther 9:1–10.

1. What was to have happened on the thirteenth day of Adar?

2. What happened instead?

3. What happened to the sons of Haman (9:6–10)?

4. Why was that important?

5. Did the Jews kill their enemies?

6. Why were the Jews able to overcome their enemies (9:2–3)?

    a.

    b.

7. What does "fear of the Jews" mean?

8. Why had fear of the Jews fallen on all the people (8:11)?

When we accept Christ's invitation of forgiveness and Lordship in our lives, we become a daughter of the King—the ultimate God of everything!

Become a Child of God

How can we become a child of God?

1. Read John 6:44 and 2 Peter 3:9. What can we learn from these two verses?

   a.

   b.

2. Read Romans 3:23.
3. Read Romans 6:23.

   The sin of Adam and Eve brought two types of death on the earth:
   a. *Physical death: now everything—all animals, all plants, and all people—would grow old and die (Romans 8:19–23).*
   b. *Spiritual death: the relationship of love and trust was broken by man's disobedience.*

4. Read Romans 5:8.

5. Read John 3:16. What two truths do we learn from this verse?

   a.

b.

Believe is the verb pisteuo; *it denotes doing, an activity.*[36] *Thus, true belief is not just an accepting of God's redemptive act as truth. Rather, it is "a loving, self-abandoning commitment that constantly draws one near to the Lord Jesus Christ in spiritual intimacy."*[37]

6. So how does a person enter into this life of faith? Read the following two scriptures to discover the first step a person should take after believing and wanting Christ to be their Lord.

   a. Read John 3:5–6.

   b. Read Acts 2:38.

7. Read Romans 6:2b–4. What is the significance of baptism?

Benefits of Accepting Christ as Savior

What are the benefits of accepting Christ as Savior? Read the following scriptures and write down what you learn.

Recognize the following:[38]

   1. John 1:12

   2. 2 Corinthians 5:17

   3. 2 Peter 1:3–4

   4. 1 John 5:4

Learning to Grow in Christ

Realize that we are a work in progress.

1. Read Philippians 2:12–13.

2. Who is involved in this work in progress?

    Growing in Christ involves us cooperating with God, allowing Him to transform us. This involves two parts: God's part and our part.

    a. My Part
        Read the following scriptures and write down what God would have you do to grow in Him.

        1) 2 Timothy 3:16–17

        2) Luke 18:1

        3) John 14:15

        4) Romans 6:12–14

        5) Hebrews 12:1–11

        6) John 15:4

        7) Ephesians 4:11–16

8) Romans 8:14; Ephesians 5:17–18

b. God's Part
Read and write down what God does for us after He has drawn us to Him and we have become His.

1) Colossians 1:13–14

2) Romans 8:38–39

3) Matthew 6:25–33

4) Matthew 7:7–11

5) 2 Timothy 3:16

6) 1 Corinthians 12:4–11

7) John 14:16–18

8) Hebrews 4:14–16

9) Hebrews 12:1–11

10) Ephesians 1:13–14

God wants us to come to know Him so well that we are aware of His presence and are talking with Him throughout each day!

Lesson 17

Victors!

Let's finish Esther and then look at our relationship with God through the lens of the third chapter of Colossians and James 4:7–8. The Apostle Paul succinctly summarized within Colossians 3 the concepts needed to live a victorious Christian life on this earth.

The Amalekites, Enemies of the Jews, Eliminated

Read Esther 9:1–16.

1. Did the Jews defend themselves and kill their enemies?

2. Did they plunder their enemies' goods (9:10)?

3. Had they been given permission to plunder (8:11)?

4. Why did they kill their enemies but not plunder their goods?

"A rule of ancient Jewish holy war was that plunder was not to be taken. Abram (Genesis 14) had refused to accept any material reward from the king of Sodom, not wanting that wicked city to be the source of his prosperity."[39]

5. What were Esther's last two requests of the king (9:13)?

   a.

   b.

6. Why do you think she requested these two things (9:15)?

   a.

   b.

The Feast of Purim

Read Esther 9:16–32.

1. What feast was started as a result of the deliverance of the Jews from wicked Haman (9:26–28)?

2. What was the purpose of having this annual feast (9:20–32)?

3. When was it celebrated (9:17–19)?

   a. Jews in Susa:

   b. Jews in the country:

4. What things happened during the celebration (9:20–22)?

   a.

b.

c.

The Final Outcome

Read Esther 10:1–3.

Esther, the little orphaned girl, became the queen of the land and rescued her people from death. Her uncle became second in command and was respected by all.

1. Why was Mordecai great and popular?

    a.

    b.

2. Why were Mordecai and Esther able to overcome their enemy?

    a.

    b.

    c.

    d.

    e.

Victorious Christian Living

How can we walk a victorious walk of faith and be beautiful on the inside and the outside?

1. On the Outside:

    a.

    b.

    c.

    d.

    e.

    f.

    g.

2. On the Inside:

    a.

    b.

    c.

    d.

e.

f.

Victorious living does not mean that life will always adhere to our desired plans. Victorious Christian living involves developing an intimate relationship with Christ that allows us to "hear" Him throughout each day. He guides, encourages, and ministers to us with His loving presence. He helps us become overcomers through the trials of this life, and we become mature women of God whose fragrance touches others for Him.

In John 15:10–11, Jesus encouraged his disciples to keep His commandments. The promised result is that they would abide in His love. What a wonderful place to be: abiding in the encompassing, overflowing, perfect love of our Savior! He also promised that His joy would be in them, and their joy would be complete.

These are wonderful promises! If we develop this relationship of love and obedience with God, we will abide in the unbounded love of our Savior and have His joy filling our hearts!

Develop a Vibrant Relationship with Christ

1. Read Colossians 3:1–17 to discover a short synopsis of how to develop a vibrant relationship with Christ. Write down what you learn from these scriptures.

   a. Colossians 3:1–2

   b. Colossians 3:3–4

   c. Colossians 3:5–9

   This is how we "work out our salvation" with "God working in us" (Philippians 2:12–13). He gently convicts. We confess, repent, and ask for His help to overcome that area of sin. Then through the Holy Spirit, He empowers us to overcome!

d. Colossians 3:12, 14

e. Colossians 3:13

f. Colossians 3:15

We need to "take our thoughts captive" (2 Corinthians 10:5) and
dwell on Christ's truths instead of Satan's attacks and lies.

g. Colossians 3:16a

h. Colossians 3:16b

i. Colossians 3:16c

Worship Him from your heart everywhere you go throughout your day.
You will be amazed at how it changes your entire outlook on life!

j. Colossians 3:17

2. We have one more short passage to consider that will help us in developing a victorious Christian life. Read James 4:7–8. What are we instructed to do in this scripture? Why are we to do it?

a.

b.

c.

*Allowing Christ into our hearts, and learning to listen and walk in
accord with the Holy Spirit, is what makes us beautiful.*

*As we allow Him to transform us, we will become beautiful on the inside. God's love, peace, and joy
will radiate out of us in our demeanor and actions. Then we will be truly beautiful—inside and out!*

God bless you all!

Endnotes

Lesson 1

1   VeggieTales, *Esther: The Girl Who Became Queen*, Big Idea Entertainment, LLC. TM & © 2003.Big Idea Productions, Inc.

Lesson 6

2   Mary Spillane and Christine Sherlock, *Color Me Beautiful's Looking Your Best* (Lanham, MD: Madison Books, 1965), p. 20. Used by permission.
3   Excerpts from *Color Me Beautiful* by Carole Jackson (Carole Jackson, 1987), pp. 47, 49, 51, 53. Used by permission of Ballantine Books. All rights reserved.
4   Ibid., pp. 26–27, 37.
5   Ibid., pp. 26, 37.
6   Ibid., pp. 22, 26, 32, 36–37.
7   Ibid., pp. 36–37
8   Ibid., pp. 47, 49, 51, 53.
9   Ibid., p. 56.
10 Ibid.
11 Ibid., pp. 25, 38.
12 Ibid., pp. 66–69.

Lesson 7

13 Some content taken from *Love Must Be Tough* by Dr. James Dobson. (Tyndale House Publishers, Inc., 1975, 2008) pp. 233–236. All rights reserved. Used by permission. Dr. James Dobson adapted this material from *Intimate Behavior* by Desmond Morris, pp. 74–78. Used by permission of Penguin Random House UK.
14 Ibid.
15 Ibid.
16 Ibid
17 Ibid.
18 Focus on the Family radio program, December 19, 2012 (www.focusonthefamily.com/radio). This was an interview with Dannah Gresh entitled "Helping Young Women Understand Sex." It was based on her book *What Are You Waiting For? The One Thing No One Ever Tells You About Sex.* Used by permission.
19 Ibid.
20 Ibid.
21 Ibid.
22 Ibid.

23 Ibid.

Lesson 8

24 Taken from *Zondervan NIV Study Bible* (Zondervan, 1985, 1995, 2002), p. 717. Used by permission of Zondervan, www.zondervan.com.

Lesson 9

25 Taken from *God's at War* by Kyle Idleman (Kyle Idleman, 2013), p. 123. Used by permission of Zondervan, www.zondervan.com.

Lesson 13

26 www.goodreads.com/.../8308- thou-hast-made-us-for-thyself- Augustine.

27 Henry T. Blackaby and Claude King, *Experiencing God* (Nashville: LifeWay Press, 1990), pp. 93–94. Used by permission.

28 Taken from *Zondervan NIV Study Bible* (Zondervan, 1985, 1995, 2002), p. 397. Used by permission of Zondervan, www.zondervan.com.

29 Henry T. Blackaby, and Claude King, *Experiencing God,* pp. 83–84, 87, 93– 95, 105. Used by permission.

Lesson 14

30 Mary Spillane and Christine Sherlock, *Color Me Beautiful's Looking Your Best* (Lanham, MD: Madison Books, 1965), pp. 69–85. Used by permission.

31 Ibid., pp. 70–72.

32 Ibid., p. 83.

33 Ibid., p. 80.

34 Ibid., p. 82–85.

35 Ibid., p. 70–79.

Lesson 16

36 Taken from *Life in the Spirit Bible* (Life Publishers International, 1992), p. 1597.

37 Ibid.

38 Taken from *Harper Study Bible* (Harper & Row, 1962), p. 1588. Used by permission of Zondervan, www.zondervan.com.

Lesson 17

39 Taken from *The NIV Archaeological Study Bible* (International Bible Society 1973, 1978, 1984), p. 728. Used by permission of Zondervan, www.zondervan.com.

Printed in the United States
By Bookmasters